California
ELEPHANT SEALS

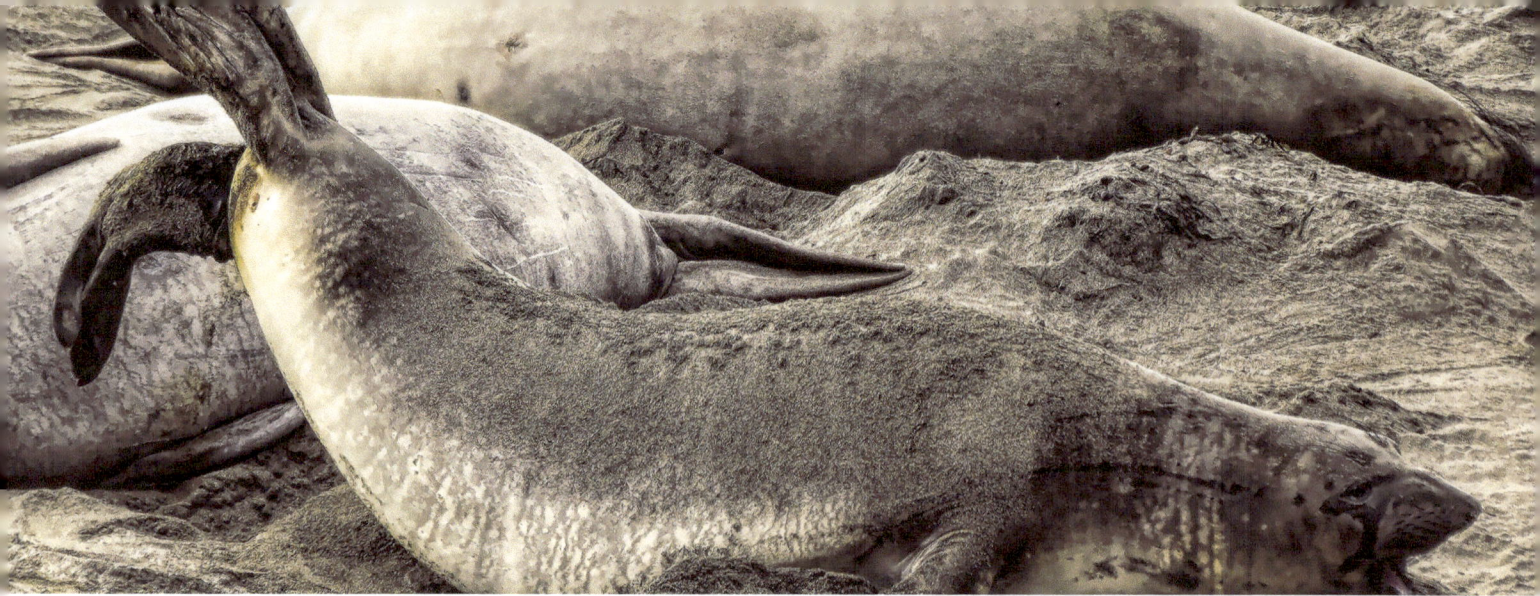

California Elephant Seals

ISBN: 978-0-9826064-8-3
Content by Elisabeth Haug
Published by Sharing Magic Moments   (760)805-8651   Info@EHaug.com

FASCINATING, AMAZING, and INTRIGUING are some of the words most often used by elephant seal connoisseurs. Newbies will understand why once they, too, get a close look at these primeval apparitions.

More than a million people from all over the world flock to the E-seals' California rookeries every year. Many of these enthusiasts have made it a tradition to come back several times annually to marvel at the spectacles. The beach scene is constantly changing depending on the season.

The species is thought to be named for it's size and the long trunk like noses of the adult males. Mature elephant seal bulls weigh in at about 5000 pounds and look like crosses between Loch Ness Monsters, dinosaurs, alligators, and giant sloths. Surprisingly, they are actually cute even though they are terribly ugly.

The females and the juveniles of both sexes look more like normal seals and have dog like noses. Adult females weigh between 1000 and 1600 pounds. Newborn pups weigh approximately 80 pounds and weaned pups 300 pounds.

E-seals can dive more than a mile and stay under water for up to 2 hours at a time. When resting on the beach, they can hold their breath while sleeping for up to 30 minutes.

The female E-seals feed mainly on squid. The males also enjoy squid, but tend more towards vacuuming the ocean floor for bottom fish.

On the beach, the seals have an active social life with clear body language and strict rules for what they consider acceptable behavior. In the ocean each seal is on his own. They are not antisocial. Hunting solo is merely more efficient for them.

Newcomers to viewing thousands of huge, wild animals dozing companionably together on the beach are generally impressed by the sight. Judging by what they see, many first time visitors believe the seals lead a cushy life. But, once the E-seal docents give them their spiel, people realize nothing is farther from the truth. Although the individual E-seal appears content, the life of the species is amazingly adventurous and grueling, at best.

E-seals spend about 20% of their time on the beach and 80% in the water. Their life is one of contradictions. For them it is either:

- Abundance or scarcity
- Feast or famine
- Ocean or beach
- Isolation or over crowding
- Extreme vigor or sleep

The seals travel (commute) at least 10,000 miles a year. The males' hunting grounds are in the vicinity of the Aleutian Islands in Alaska. The females' are a tad southwest from the males' haunts. Both locations are approximately 2,500 miles away from the beach homes in California. Each seal makes the journey to-and-fro twice a year.

On an average beach sojourns last between 4 and 6 weeks. The adults birth and breed on land here in the winter. In the spring and summer the seals come ashore to molt —change their coats. Additionally, the juveniles come here in the fall merely to sleep, socialize, and build up the density of their bones.

The E-seals eat little or nothing while on the beach, And while traveling they do not slow down to forage for any extended time. Because of this, they have to make up for lost time when they finally arrive at their hunting grounds. Once situated, they dive and hunt 24 hours a day in order to pack on the pounds.

Those E-seal males who live to old age can reach 15 years. Females sometimes live till their early twenties.

But while E-seals are relatively safe on land, many dangers lurk for them in the ocean. It is believed that about 60% die before they are 4 years old.
- Predators—Great white sharks and orcas are the most serious
- Starvation leading to hypothermia
- Entanglements and contamination due to human negligence
- Accidents to pups and weaners. Pup death is most often the result of:
    1. Preweaned pups being separated from their mothers.
    2. Pups being washed out in violent surf during high tides.
    3. Pups being attacked by cranky females other than their mothers.
    4. Pups being run over by posturing or fighting males.

It is believed that seals can sleep-swim on their downward dives. But considering the dangers surrounding them, that type of sleep is probably not very restful. Also, it has no REM phase.

We still have much to learn about the E-seals. And what we believe we know is regularly challenged as newer information is gathered.

Whereas we can—with some difficulty—follow the E-seals on the beach, it is nearly impossible to watch them at sea.

Research has been done by tagging them and by electronic monitoring, but doing so on a continuous major scale is cost prohibitive.

Pups are tagged at several rookeries. Each location has its own identifying color. San Miguel Island has yellow tags; Año Nuevo Green, and Piedras Blancas white.

About 5% of the pups—about 250— are tagged each year at Piedras Blancas. A comparable percentage are tagged at Año Nuevo. The biggest problem with the tags is that they are difficult to see—let alone read—from an appropriate distance.

The picture at the bottom of the opposite page show one of the electronic devices that have been used to chart the E-seals on their yearly travels.

The story of the northern elephant seal is one of amazing survival skills! Before our time, E-seals made the islands of Baja in Northern Mexico their beach home. There, in the 1800's, they were discovered by delighted whalers.

It was much safer for the whalers to hunt the beached seals than to search for whales, chase them, and fight them. It was also easier, quicker, and more economical. A crew with guns could kill a whole beach full of dozing E-seals in a single swoop. Additionally, the E-seal blubber is of superior quality both for lubrication and lamp oil.

By 1880, the northern elephant seal was believed to be extinct. Fortunately— about a decade later—it was discovered by scientists on an unrelated expedition that a small, hidden colony of about 100 had escaped the slaughter.

That news created great excitement and in 1922 Mexico placed a ban on murdering the seals. The United States followed suit in 1927.

Today—less than 150 years later—the 100 or so E-seal survivors have multiplied into a population of close to 200,000. E-seals tend to return to the beaches where they were born and many still beach on the original islands in Baja. Nevertheless, the most adventurous of the species discovered the California coast and have established three major rookeries here:
- The Santa Barbara Channel Islands
- Año Nuevo Island and Año Nuevo State Reserve
- Piedras Blancas

Overcrowding in their original territories has certainly been a factor in their increase of venue. But equally important was probably that their northward move lessened their migration by about 500 miles each way—close to 20% of the total distance. Considering the short time they have at their hunting grounds between journeys that must be an important factor.

When scoping out a new beach home e-seals appear to look for moderate tides and wide, gently sloping, sandy beaches. Rocky tide pools and massive, dense kelp beds are also important as a protection for the weaners against sharks and other marine predators.

Seal pups can't swim or dive when they are born. They need to teach themselves to do so once their mothers have left them. The abandoned weaners gather in large groups and lead a Peter Pan like life.

Previously, E-seals preferred beaching on islands far away from humans and other large land predators. That made the Santa Barbara Channel Islands an obvious choice for their initial California hangout decision. These islands are a nature paradise.

The first wave of E-seals arrived here in the early 1950's. Nowadays San Miguel Island, San Nicolas Island, and Santa Rosa Island combined are the beach homes of close to 100,000 E-seals.

The Santa Barbara Channel Islands are peaceful. And fish and other seafoods are abundant in the surrounding waters. The islands are the favorite breeding grounds for many marine birds and mammals including pelicans and sea lions.

As interesting as it would be for E-seal enthusiasts to visit the rookeries on the islands, the logistics are too difficult to arrange for the average sightseer.

San Nicolas Island is controlled by the U.S. Navy. Flights land on Santa Rosa Island all year, but the E-seals are a 16 mile hike away from the landing strip. On some dates during the late summer, a few ferries go from Ventura to San Miguel Island where molting E-seals can be viewed in the harbor area.

In 1955—a few years after the seals annexed the Santa Barbara Channel Islands—a few E-seals came to the tiny Año Nuevo Island which is known for its now defunct lighthouse. You are not allowed to visit the island, itself, any more but you can view the E-seals at the adjacent Año Nuevo State Reserve. It is located on Highway 1 in Pescadero about 30 miles north of Santa Rosa. When the E-seal population at the island rookery grew too large, some of the seals moved to the reserve. It became the E-seals' first mainland home. Their number at this rookery varies but it is estimated that in most years about 2000 pups are born here.

E-seals have created considerable interest in scientific as well as layman circles. Most of the northern elephant seal research has been done with the help of the nearby UC Santa Cruz.

Visiting the E-seals at Año Nuevo is fun and doable for most. The trails are easy and beautifully maintained. The docents are friendly and knowledgeable, and chances are that you will encounter other types of wildlife as you go.

With his pleasant manner and great information, Ed Lambing—the docent in the photo above—made my friends' and my Año Nuevo tour an enjoyable and memorable experience. We booked our tour at http://anonuevo.reserveamerica.com/

The following information is quoted from the park's website:

 "The park offers guided walks lead by volunteer docent naturalist to see the elephant seals in their natural habitat inside the Natural Preserve. Año Nuevo docents go through extensive training and are highly knowledgeable in the natural and cultural history of the park. These walks begin December 15 and continue every day until March 31, except December 25 and January 24 & 25. To view the seals during this period, you must be on a guided walk.

These popular three-to-four mile walks over rolling sand dunes last 2.5 hours and are considered moderately strenuous. They operate daily from early morning to mid-afternoon, rain or shine. Reservations are recommended for these guided walks. Visitors who are late for their guided walk will forfeit their reservations."

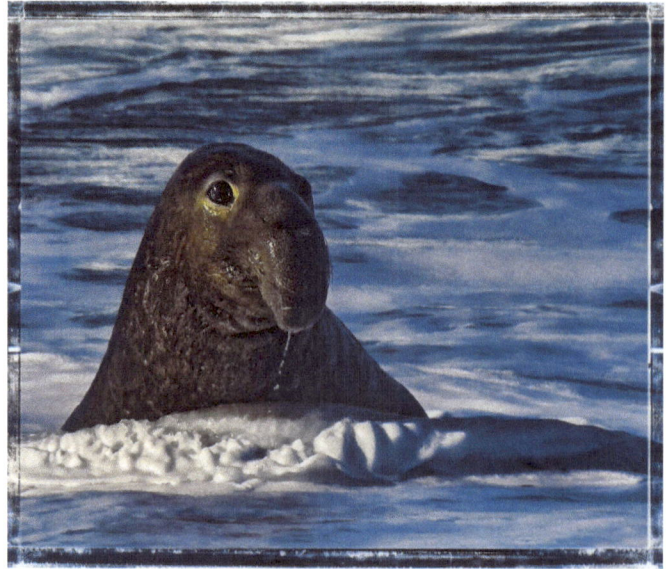

The newest and possibly fastest growing colony is Piedras Blancas. It is located on the mainland adjacent to Highway 1 about 45 miles north of San Luis Obispo. It is in the neighborhood of San Simeon and Hearst Castle.

Piedras Blancas is named for the series of distinct white rocks right off the coast. They are a favorite of pelicans, cormorants, and sea lions.

Just like Año Nuevo and the Santa Barbara Channel Islands, Piedras Blancas is the site of an abandoned lighthouse. On November 25, 1990 staff looked down from the tower and were astounded to see 11 E-seals lounging on the beach below.

Since then—in the short span of 25 years—the population of the rookery has risen to 17,000+. Currently about 4,700 pups are born here each year.

From covering a single short stretch, the colony now calls a 4.5 mile range of sandy coves and beaches its own. The most well known and most easily accessible part of that shoreline makes up the official E-seal vista. It covers the beaches preferred by the seals. Here, you can watch an abundance of them year around.

The turnout has a huge parking lot and is easy to find. Signs show you the way.

Piedras Blancas is the only place in the world where you can watch E-seals only a few feet from your parked car. The site has about half a mile of great viewing boardwalks and wide gravel trails.

Capable, enthusiastic docents are provided by *Friends of the Elephant Seal*— a non-government organization with the mission to educate the public about the elephant seal.

E-seals own their beaches on a timeshare basis. Each group comes in from the ocean at a scheduled time. Individuals visit their chosen rookery twice a year normally for a period of about a month to six weeks every time.

Not all of the seals in a category come in at exactly the same time so the groups tend to overlap. Some individuals miss the memo altogether and mix their schedules up completely.

No two years are identical but the E-seals' calendar looks something like this:

- **April through May:** Adult females and juveniles (1-4 years) come in to molt. Some sub-adult males arrive in May.
- **June:** Sub-adult males (4-7 years) come in to molt.
- **July through August :** Adult males arrive and molt. Sub-adult male stragglers remain.
- **Late August through November:** Fall haul-out—juveniles of both sexes arrive to hangout together, develop their bone density, and rest.
- **December through March:** Birthing and breeding season—adult males, pregnant and nursing mothers, newborn pups and weaners.
- **March through mid April:** Weaned pups live a Peter Pan like existence almost alone on the beach.

All E-seals need to molt once a year—shed their old coat and grow a new one.

Because the water they swim in is only about 40 degrees fahrenheit—too cold for them to molt—they have to come ashore to bask in the sun. When they arrive they look like rag-muffins, but when they leave their new fur is shiny and sleek.

April and May are the most crowded months of the year on the beach. This is when both the adult females and all the juveniles come in. The seals lie in big piles—sometimes even on top of one another.

It is the only time of the year when the females can truly sleep without any responsibilities or concerns.

Like other teenyboppers, the juveniles want to party and compete. Whereas this initially causes conflict with the females, peace returns as the juveniles are chased away and relegated to the least desirable areas. Here they can play and spar to their hearts' content in and out of the water.

The sub adult males begin to arrive towards the end of May as the females and juveniles are leaving. They bicker and spar, like to make trouble, and are boisterous and full of themselves.

When the adult females put them in their place, they turn around and take their frustration out on those younger than themselves. Whereas most E-seals are patient with one another, a fair number of the sub adult males are bullies.

In July and August, the adult males start arriving. Like young males of other species the sub adults relish to antagonize their elders. Often a severe look from one of their superiors is enough to send them scuttling to safety. But now and then an over confident sub adult goes too far, and needs to be pursued and chased as a result. In the worst case scenario he receives one or more sharp bites in his loin region—the tender part of his back.

The "big males" use their sojourn on the beach to rest and to socialize. Without any females to distract them, these gentle giants often doze in one big heap. But they never forget to be competitive.

They use this relaxed time of year to establish each individual's place in the pecking order. They hold the annual E-seal Sumo Wrestling Championships, so to speak.

The males challenge each other to their hearts' content. During this time of the year you will see more fighting than at any other. It is seldom serious, but by the end of their stay every male has a good idea of his place in the hierarchy.

This arrangement saves considerable energy and grief during the next breeding season when male fighting is dangerous for whichever pups get in the way.

Towards the end of August almost all of the adult males are gone and the juveniles of both sexes begin drizzling in.

The next months are the slowest and least entertaining of the year. The seals are less active then and their numbers on the beach are smaller than at any other time.

The young seals are worn and tired from their quest to survive and flourish during their journeying.

The pups of the year have learned much and become less innocent. The ocean voyage they have just returned from

was their first. Just having survived its dangers and obstacles means they are winners. A large number of their contemporaries have succumbed.

The youngsters on the beach spend considerable time sleeping, yet few refuse when other youngsters invite them to participate in sparring matches. There is still plenty to look at for you if you have scheduled this period for your visit.

Everybody looks forward to the excitement of the birthing and breeding season. We are all fascinated by the arrival of new life.

Almost all of the juveniles have left when the first adult males arrive in the beginning of December. Those youngsters who have come in late and don't feel ready to leave the beach yet avoid being chastised by fleeing to rocky, more remote beaches.

One does not need to be an expert to recognize the adult E-seal males. Their size, their long bulbous noses, their tough, pink scuffed chest shield, and their frequent challenging bellows give them away.

Upon arrival, the first thing a male does is to stake a claim to the best area he can get—either one that is vacant or one that is "owned" by a lesser male whom he can displace.

Winning a territory does not mean that a male will be able to keep it for any length of time. But here—just like in the human world—possession is nine tenths of the law. The first pregnant E-seal females come ashore around the middle of December. They, too, seek to settle in the most desirable available locations. But whereas males evaluate a location by the quantity and status of the females it attracts, it is the area's suitability for raising a pup that matters to the pregnant mothers.

E-seal females have one pup a year. Their conception rate is unusually high. Yet, so far no twin births have been documented.

The females approach the shore one by one. Running the gauntlet of amorous males can be a daunting experience.

Females give birth within the first 10 days they are on land. If a female decides she no longer likes the location she initially chose, or if she is harassed by stronger females, she can swim to another beach at any time until her pup is born.

E-seals are very attuned to each others' voices. During the first few minutes of a pup's life mother and child repeatedly call to one another.

By bonding in this way, they are always later able to recognize each other on the crowded beach.

You can hear what various E-seals sound like at this site:
parks.ca.gov/?paged=1116

One of the most exciting experiences one can have during this time of year is witnessing a birth. Below are some of the signs to look for if you would like to catch a pup entering the world

First: Realize that once you look away from the seal of your choice you may not be able to recognize her when you return your gaze to where you thought she was.

Second: Begin by looking for a female that does not have a pup next to her and:

- Is showing a different behavior than the seals surrounding her. All seals exhibit several of the signs listed below ever so often. So if many are doing something odd chances are that it is not a crucial sign.
- Water breaking is always a good start. But it does not guarantee the birth is imminent.
- The mother-to-be becomes restless and agitated. It may look as if she has a bulge close to her hind flippers. Females, however, are often uncomfortable when they first come on land. Who wouldn't be with a big lump inside the belly and suddenly experiencing gravity for the first time in months?
- Delivering females often start flipping sand, but so may many of the other seals to cool down.
- Shortly before the delivery, most females start looking about and calling their unborn pup. They may bury their heads in the sand and/or start snapping at surrounding mothers and pups. They often make circles around themselves.
- The biggest deterrent to catching the birth is that the mothers-to-be tend to move around. At the last minute they may block your view by turning their heads towards you rather than their tails. Or they may move behind other seals.
- Some females lift their hind flippers up high when it comes time to push. Others don't.

The islands of San Clemente, Santa Barbara, San Nicholas and San Miguel produce approximately 81% of US born pups. About 11% are born at Piedras Blancas. The last 8% are born at Año Nuevo.

Adult males use vocalization in a way similar to that of mothers and pups. When a male is challenged by the roar of someone he has been confronted by before, he immediately recognizes the aggressor's below and knows exactly where in the hierarchy the specific individual belongs.

Research was done to document this useful ability. First the bellows of a number of males were recorded. Then they were played through loud speakers on the beaches where they were recorded. The voices of the lesser males created little attention, but when the challenges of the beach masters were played, the result was commotion. When the same tapes were played at other rookeries where the taped males were unknown, the reaction was minimal.

If you have missed the actual event, seagulls descending from everywhere will alert you to recent births. As soon as a female has passed her placenta, the gulls will squawk and swoop down to eat it.

When you first observe this onslaught of gulls, you may feel affronted by their aggression and lack of tact. But the birds have no intention of hurting the newborns and it is their vigilance as cleanup crews that keep the beach clean and disease free.

The pups are wrinkled and skinny when they are born, but their thirst and their mothers' plentiful, rich milk allow them to swiftly pack on the pounds. The milk—rich from the start—increases gradually in fat content. At the end of their nursing period it has become about 53%.

The newborns weigh between 60 and 100 pounds. When their mothers have to leave them a scant four weeks later their skins have been filled out. They are blimps and hopefully weigh 300 pounds or more.

Weaners—weaned pups whose mothers have left the beach—often try to make up for their loss by attempting to sneak meals from other females. This is seldom a productive solution. The accosted females have sharp teeth and show no reservations about using them savagely to make their displeasure with the thievery absolutely clear.

One of the worst things that can happen to not yet weaned E-seal pups is to be separated from their mothers and not be able to return to them. Unfortunately this is common when the beach is at its most crowded. Even if they find each other again, mother and child often have a gauntlet of irritated females keeping them apart.

Nursing females resent other females moving into their territory and do their best to fight invaders off even when the intruder is merely trying to get to her pup. Younger, weaker females generally don't have the courage to break through the fracas.

At times becoming lost spells a slow death. A pup needs every drop of his mother's milk in order to grow fat enough to survive the upcoming year. In other instances the lost pup is taken in by a female whose own pup has been lost. Some of these adoptive mothers—like the one in the photo above—go overboard. She is nursing five. The most I have seen is six.

Another danger to the pups—especially the newborns—is being run over by rampaging males challenging each other or even worse fighting on top of them.

Generally the pups survive the encounters and are none the worse for the wear. A good consequence is that they become aware of the dangers of others and learn to get out of the way of trouble. This insight and the reflexes developed must be helpful for them later when they are exposed to predators in the ocean. Nonetheless, being steamrolled by a 5000 pound giant is not fun and accidents resulting in death do happen—especially to the very young.

Yet another threat to E-seal pups is being washed out by the tide.

Not only will they be separated from their mothers in the confusion of high waves, but they haven't mastered the ways of the ocean, yet, and easily drown.

Some years have higher tides than others. The greatest dangers are when high tides and high surf occur simultaneously.

Unfortunately, it is the younger, weaker, and more inexperienced females who are pushed closest to the ocean.

When her pup is 24 to 28 days old, the mother will go into estrous and be receptive to being rebred. Once that has taken place, it is time for her to wean her pup and return to the ocean. She has lost about a third of her body weight and needs to eat again to preserve her strength.

While she is inside the confines of the harem, the dominant male—the big cheese—will keep her to himself and frighten other males away. But once she heads to the ocean, she normally loses his protection and mating with her becomes a free for all.

In many cases, the female welcomes the extra attention from the younger males and lets herself

be mated with one or more before she—alone once again— swims away towards her hunting grounds.

At other times the scenario is less idyllic. Being in the middle of the confusion—with too many males fighting over her—she just wants to get away. But this is often easier said for her than done. Some raunchy males will pursue females way out into the water and try to prevent them from getting away by herding them back to the shore.

Towards the end of February almost all of the adult females have left and only the wieners—oops weaners—and a few die-hard adult males are left on the beaches.

One would expect the weaners to feel abandoned, worried, and depressed. Instead, they appear to enjoy their new freedom from the bossy adults. They begin to lead a Peter Pan like life playing hard and sleeping it off next to one another in huge piles. They learn to master the water—swim and dive.

They yip and yap excitedly, spar and play. Learning by example they—day by day—proudly teach each other the new tricks they have just learned.

They prefer to assemble near lagoons and fresh water streams. Here they are safe and there are plenty of fish for them to practice their eye to mouth coordination on.

Towards the end of March or early April, the weaners begin to feel confident enough to take on a larger scene.

One by one, they set to sea heading out towards their hunting grounds far away. Doing so would be a daunting experience for anyone, yet these innocent babies face all their new challenges without a whimper, learning as they go.

Some succumb to the dangers, but far more make it back to the beach in the fall.

Elisabeth Haug

Visit my website: **EHaug.com** To view more of my photography and other projects.

A B O U T   T H E   P H O T O G R A P H E R

I have always loved life and our planet—nature, people, animals, learning, art, fun, and action.

I was born in Denmark, but when I was a child my parents moved often, trying out new countries.

By the time I moved back to Denmark at age 16 to start engineering school, I had attended 17 different schools.

Later, I became hooked on the Icelandic Horse—the small, sturdy pony that carried the Vikings and Genghis Khan in earlier times.

Even later, in 1978 my family and I moved to California, flying in a DC6 filled with horses.

Pioneering the breed in the United States proved both challenging and exciting. In order to succeed I pursued many horse disciplines including working with cattle and endurance racing, I participated in the Rose Parade several times.

Simultaneously—in order to improve my people skills—I worked on well-known motivator Tony Robbins' seminar support team for a number of years.

Now retired from breeding and training horses, I am able to dedicate myself 100% to my other passions—photography, writing, and publishing

One of my latest results is this book. I hope you enjoy browsing its content as much as I have enjoyed creating it. Until we meet again, may the road come up to meet you and the force of the E-seal be with you!